WASHINGTON PLACE

"Simply the most moving and inspiring piece of theater I saw all year. It also reminded me of just how wonderfully intimate theater can be... Set against the ominous horrors of the Triangle Shirtwaist Factory fire of 1911, David Brendan Hopes' new play, *Washington Place,* tells a story of hope and inspiration about the workers within that doomed building. The Magnetic Theatre has something special on its hands in this great play by a local author [about] a day in the life of women who are not allowed to dream of more or aspire to better lives. Some accept it, some protest it. There is no sense of their impending doom, which makes what is to come all the more unsettling. We get to know, and develop an affection for, these women and their plight. The show is powerful. It reminds us of the sacrifices of those who died over a century ago. It is also a cautionary tale to warn us that such struggles are still playing out in our world today. This is what theater can and should be."

—Jeff Messer, *Mountain Xpress*

Many have heard about the devastating Triangle Shirtwaist Factory fire on New York City's Lower East Side in 1911, and about the important labor laws enacted in its deadly wake. But no one knows much, if anything, about the lives of the young women caught up in this tragedy. Now David Brendan Hopes beautifully imagines their lives for us, bringing us their passions, hopes, and dreams, as well as their songs and laughter, in an effervescent, moving world premiere.

ALSO PUBLISHED BY THE SUBLIME THEATER & PRESS

American Arcade
by Steven Samuels

My Crazy My Love
by John Crutchfield

WASHINGTON PLACE

DAVID BRENDAN HOPES

THE SUBLIME THEATER & PRESS
Asheville, NC

Washington Place
Copyright © 2021 by David Brendan Hopes

Published by The Sublime Theater & Press, Inc.
49 Faircrest Road, Asheville, NC 28804-1848
ss@thesublimetheater.org

The Sublime Theater & Press, Inc. is a 501(c)(3) tax-exempt organization.

All rights reserved. Except for brief passages quoted in newspaper, magazine, radio, television, or online reviews, no part of this book may be reproduced in any form or by any means, electronic or mechanical, including photocopying or recording, or by an information storage and retrieval system, without permission in writing from the publisher.

Professionals and amateurs are hereby warned that this material, being fully protected under the Copyright Laws of the United States of America and all other countries of the Berne and Universal Copyright Conventions, is subject to a royalty. All rights including, but not limited to, professional, amateur, recording, motion picture, recitation, lecturing, public reading, radio and television broadcasting, online presentation, and the rights of translation into foreign languages, are expressly reserved. Particular emphasis is placed on the question of readings and all uses of this book by educational institutions. Inquiries concerning production rights for this play should be addressed to the publisher.

ISBN 978-1-952720-12-3 (Hardcover)
ISBN 978-1-952720-04-8 (Paperback)
ISBN 978-1-952720-05-5 (E-book)

First edition, May 2021

Washington Place was first presented by The Magnetic Theatre at 375 Depot Street, Asheville, NC, on November 5, 2015.

Written by David Brendan Hopes
Directed by Steven Samuels
Costume, Set, and Prop Design by Kayren McKnight
Lighting Design by Jason Williams
Sound Design by Mary Zogzas
Hair Design by Sandy McDaniel
Choreography by Kristi DeVille
Board Operation/Stage Management by Marissa Mello

CAST
(in order of appearance)
Providenza Panno…Terry Darakjy
Avi Nussbaum…Allen T. Law
Gussie Bierman…Valerie Meiss
Yetta Goldstein…Samantha Stewart
Essie…Devyn Ray
Lucia Maltese…Emmalie Handley
Rosaria Maltese…Sophie Yates

TIME: March 25, 1911

PLACE: The Triangle Shirtwaist Company, 23-29 Washington Place, Greenwich Village

CAST (in order of appearance)
AVI NUSSBAUM, kid with his first job, 15
GUSSIE BIERMAN, devout Jewish working girl, 22
YETTA GOLDSTEIN, radicalized Jewish working girl, 20
ESSIE, romantic Jewish working girl, 19
ROSARIA MALTESE, Italian, 14
LUCIA MALTESE, her sister, 20
PROVIDENZA PANNO, Italian supervisor, 48

NOTES ON THE PLAY: This is a true story. The Triangle Shirtwaist Company burned on March 25, 1911, with the loss of 146 lives, mostly women, mostly through the gross and callous negligence of the factory management. The names chosen for this dramatic presentation are the names of actual victims and the ages their actual ages, though the characterization is purely speculative and nothing to do with how they may actually have lived their lives. Avi is not listed among the victims because he survived. This information should be withheld from the audience, not because they won't know it but because they should be allowed to absorb the characters' day without intrusive reference to the end of it.

Most of the workers at the Triangle factory were non-English speakers. The play calls upon the imagination to suppose that conversation among the Jewish girls is in Yiddish, and conversation including both the Jewish girls and the Italian girls is foreign speakers communicating in English.

The girls talk while they work the big industrial sewing machines in pantomime. There are photos of the workrooms, but the layout is not very conducive to theater sightlines, so a creative reinterpretation is probably necessary.

WASHINGTON PLACE

SCENE ONE

The Triangle Shirtwaist Company, 23-29 Washington Place, Greenwich Village, on the morning of March 25, 1911. The room is a textile sweatshop full of sewing and cutting machines on benches, with full scrap bins lying about, and lengths of cloth hanging here and there from the ceiling or other projections. It is, of course, a firetrap. Lights come up to indicate early morning.

PROVIDENZA PANNO enters. What she does will depend somewhat on the set design. She gets the room ready for the day. She opens a few high windows for air, maybe, inspects this or that. She picks up a piece of cloth, sniffs it, makes a face, tosses it in a waste bin. She dusts here, checks a plug there. She goes from machine to machine making ready. She may turn a few on and off to see if they're working properly. She may find an apple core or a piece of personal property which she stows properly. When she is done, she exits. The stage is still for a moment.

AVI enters, pushing a broom. He sweeps up mounds of scraps and junk, dumps them in the big scrap bins. He is trying to learn Italian for his new girlfriend; in this case, the months of the year, which he mispronounces in a particularly musical way—GenNArio. FABrio. Marzo. APril, MAggiO—*which he repeats until he realizes it's the opening passage of "Oh, You Beautiful Doll," a huge hit of 1911. He grins and goes with it. When he gets downstage, finished with the sweeping, he lets fly with a genuine vaudeville song-and-dance routine. Alone, he can ham it up.*

AVI: *(Looking at the mess, more melodrama distress than real distress)* Oy, *schmutzig*! Messy girls day after day. What kind of life is this? *(Sweeping, squint-eyed with concentration)* Gennario. Fabrio. Marzo, Aprille, Maggio... *(Repeats, with almost unconscious rhythm of the popular song)* GennNArio, FABrio, MarzoAPrilMAggiO... *(Pause, may repeat, getting it, now musical, accompanied by rhythmic strokes of the broom)* GenNArio, FABrio, MarzoAPrilMAggiO... *(He looks around, sees nobody. He begins to sing, maybe dancing with his broom)*

Honey dear, when you're near,
Just turn out the light and then come over here,
Nestle close, up to my side,
My heart's on fire, with love's desire.

In my arms, rest complete,
I never thought that life could ever be so sweet,
Till I met you some time ago,
But now I know I love you so.

Oh! you beautiful doll,
You great big beautiful doll!
Let me put my arms about you,
I could never live without you;

Oh! you beautiful doll,
You great big beautiful doll!
If you ever leave me how my heart will ache,
I want to hug you but I fear you'd break.
Oh, oh, oh, oh,
Oh, you beautiful doll!

> *He vamps as he exits, swinging the broom. After a few moments of silence there's the groan of a distant elevator, then the sound of two women coming down a long corridor. The one door is quite narrow, so YETTA and GUSSIE collide and jam together in it—a slapstick moment. One elaborately withdraws and waves the other through. They go to opposite sides of the room, take off and stash their coats, settle, begin threading the needles of the sewing machines.*

GUSSIE: *Gevalt!*

YETTA: What?

GUSSIE: Nothing. Here again, is all.

YETTA: It's the most we can ask.

GUSSIE: Nice day.

YETTA: So far.

GUSSIE: The elevator smells.

YETTA: It can smell all it wants as long as it works.

GUSSIE: *(Sitting, slipping off her shoes and rubbing her feet for a moment)* Ach, these shoes!

YETTA: They're pretty.

GUSSIE: I know they're pretty. They're the ruin of me because of it. I saw them on a trash can. Six days now and you're just noticing.

YETTA: I try not to look at the floor. Who puts shoes like that on the trash can?

GUSSIE: Fifth Avenue.

YETTA: Oh.

GUSSIE: I lifted them off the trash. I put them on. I loved them. It didn't matter for the first block or so that they wouldn't have fit me when I was twelve. I loved them, they didn't love me back.

YETTA: For beauty we make sacrifices.

GUSSIE: Rich women must all have tiny feet.

YETTA: Because they never use them.

GUSSIE: Little mouse feet—

YETTA: Scurrying in and out of the stores...carrying their little mouse packages...nibbling their tiny mouse lunches with all the lettuce...

Yetta makes a nibbly mouse face. They both laugh, quiet down, work silently for a moment.

GUSSIE: I am sorry to make fun of people. Even rich people. Rich people have their problems too.

YETTA: I'm sure they would say so.

Pause.

GUSSIE: We must come on the same train.

YETTA: Why must we?

GUSSIE: We always arrive at the same time.

YETTA: All this time working in the same place you'd think we'd see each other on the train.

GUSSIE: You take the front, I take the back—we might never see each other if we didn't meet in that doorway.

YETTA: Isn't that typical?

GUSSIE: The thread is damp this morning.

YETTA: All the cloth is a little damp. Did it rain last night?

GUSSIE: All night.

YETTA: I didn't notice.

GUSSIE: Entertaining President Taft again, eh?

YETTA: He can't get enough of me.

GUSSIE: My Uncle Shlomo says President Taft is a Jew.

YETTA: Your Uncle Shlomo has an interesting perspective on a number of things.

Pause.

GUSSIE: The rain made the sky pretty.

YETTA: Did it? I didn't notice.

GUSSIE: That's because you never look at anything.

YETTA: *(Surprised)* What?

GUSSIE: Don't say "What?" at me like that. Have you ever watched yourself, Yetta? You never look in the shop windows. You never look at the people. I knew we took the same train because I saw you day after day. I waved at first but I might as well have been waving at a wall. I thought you hated me—

YETTA: No!

GUSSIE: Oh, I know it isn't that. I know now. You just didn't bother to see me. You look at the paving stones. You look at the tops of your ugly shoes. I don't know what you're looking at. Things you can't even see. And God help you if you ever try to start a conversation!

It's always "O! The plight of the poor" this and "O! Equal rights for everybody" that. You never think about anything important.

YETTA: *(Almost amused)* Well, I shall certainly try to mend my ways, Gussie.

Pause, the women working.

GUSSIE: Your shoes are not ugly. I'm sorry I said that.

Pause, the women working.

GUSSIE: Let me ask you something.

YETTA: Ask.

GUSSIE: When did they begin to pay you? How long had you worked when you got a pay packet?

YETTA: Four weeks. Four weeks of free labor while I "learned the trade" our grandmothers taught us. You have a look on you.

GUSSIE: Six for me.

YETTA: Six weeks?

GUSSIE: Yes.

YETTA: And you resent that because you're a better seamstress than me.

GUSSIE: Resent? I don't know "resent"—

YETTA: You ask for that kind of treatment because you—

GUSSIE: DON'T!

YETTA: *(Sigh)* They thought I was more likely to complain. The strike had them scared, a little, though they'd never admit it.

GUSSIE: You do complain a good deal.

YETTA: Well, that's the secret. If we joined the union, somebody would listen.

GUSSIE: And if I had wings I could fly to the moon. What happened to the mess we left last night?

YETTA: And every night.

GUSSIE: It was worse last night. I was mad. I made a worse mess. I wanted somebody to suffer.

YETTA: Elves.

GUSSIE: What? Elves?

YETTA: Like in the story—where the poor tailor has to work so hard, and the elves take pity on him and—uh—
(Gussie is clearly clueless)
Panno comes in at the crack of dawn and strokes the machines so they'll purr all day. Avi comes in and cleans up. They're both in and out before we catch our mutual train.

GUSSIE: I left that dreck for poor Avi!

YETTA: You probably did think it was elves. He's a good boy.

GUSSIE: Yes.

YETTA: Gets his work done.

GUSSIE: Why wouldn't he? He lives downstairs.

YETTA: Does he?

GUSSIE: He doesn't even have to take the train. I bet he would acknowledge me if he did.

YETTA: So will I from now on, I promise. He's cute. Did you notice?

GUSSIE: Oh, I noticed.

YETTA: Him and that Italian girl—

GUSSIE: *(Delicious gossip)* I know! Do you hear him trying to pick up bits of Italian so he can talk to her? What a *shaygets*! He could talk to me in Eskimo if he wanted to. *(Pause, change in tone)* So, how was your meeting last night?

YETTA: Don't start with me!

GUSSIE: Who's starting? I only asked.

YETTA: It was fine. Thank you for asking.

GUSSIE: Oh, so it's a big secret all of a sudden!

YETTA: I know you hate the politics and that, so why would I bring it up?

GUSSIE: As if you know what I like and don't like.

YETTA: Sorry. You should come.

GUSSIE: I should come?

YETTA: Yes.

GUSSIE: I should come to one of your meetings?

YETTA: Yes.

GUSSIE: And why is that exactly?

YETTA: It might be good for you.

GUSSIE: You never asked me before.

YETTA: I'm asking you now.

GUSSIE: You should take one of the other girls. They have time on their hands.

YETTA: I'm asking you.

GUSSIE: I should take time off from my glamorous life and go to your Socialist meeting, why is that?

YETTA: You might meet a boy.

GUSSIE: I should look for that sort of boy, heaven forbid.

YETTA: Seriously?

GUSSIE: Of course seriously.

YETTA: *(At work, not looking at Gussie)* The meetings are the beginning of awareness. Awareness is the beginning of action. In order to insure better action, we must organize!

GUSSIE: You sound like a boy reciting his Torah verse.

YETTA: You look away like a spoiled child every time somebody mentions something wrong in the world. Who told you that you had to be *satisfied*? Stamping your foot and sticking out your bottom lip are not going to improve working conditions. They're not going to get women the vote.

GUSSIE: I should vote now?

YETTA: Arguing with me all the time is not going to make Mr. Harris fix the elevators or allow us time to shove a bit of bread into our mouths at noon. Wouldn't you like a fire escape? A corridor that doesn't stink? Wouldn't you like a window of your own, that you could open and close when you wanted?

GUSSIE: On a day like this?

YETTA: Yes, on a day like this. Let rain and snow come through just so I could have a little breeze once in a while. A little noise from the street.

GUSSIE: Like there's not enough noise already from the machines—

YETTA: On a July day when we're all fainting from the heat, a little flutter of breeze. Imagine that, if you can. The balloon man crying on Washington Square.

GUSSIE: *The balloon man?*

YETTA: Do you have any imagination at all? Do you ever think of a place better than this?

GUSSIE: I think of Jerusalem.

YETTA: Good for you.

GUSSIE: Who has time for imagination when you have five younger brothers and one no-good sister who wouldn't lift a finger to put out a fire on herself? Who's going to put food on the table with me parading down 2nd Avenue with my fiancé that I should have one day God willing? I say thanks to Mr. Harris and Mr. Blanck every time I climb those stairs. I say thanks twice when the elevator's working. *(Pause)* It's not everywhere you get twelve dollars a week.

YETTA: It's not everywhere you work nine hours a day, six on Saturday, and wait six weeks to get it.

GUSSIE: They tell you that at the Socialist meetings?

YETTA: Yes they do.

GUSSIE: They're godless.

YETTA: They are not godless. Not all of them.

GUSSIE: It's just going to make you unhappy when they promise and promise and you end up with just what you have now.

YETTA: That's just it. There's no "they" anymore with us. We're not waiting on "them." We don't care what *they* promise. We're going to get it ourselves. We will accept justice graciously, take it forcibly, whatever comes first.

GUSSIE: Oh, big talk.

YETTA: See if we don't back it up. Avi comes.

GUSSIE: The cute broom boy? To the meetings?

YETTA: Yes—

GUSSIE: What a world—

YETTA: His English is good. He translates what's being said up front to the old ladies who sometimes don't understand so good.

GUSSIE: Must make their little hearts flutter. I saw him on the street without his yarmulke.

YETTA: He's just trying to fit in.

GUSSIE: You and Avi the broom boy go to your firebrand meetings and one day I'll sit under the canopy with my family all around drinking the sweet wine. Soon they'll find a husband for me. Soon I'll be out of here.

YETTA: "One day...soon...soon..."

GUSSIE: You can make fun of me all you want.

YETTA: So what if your husband is a scholar or something and you still have to work?

GUSSIE: Then that's what will happen.

YETTA: You make me tired all the time waiting for someone else to provide for you. Father, husband. Wouldn't you like to do for yourself? I mean, once or twice? What if it doesn't work out the way it's supposed to? What if you never find a husband. What then? You starve?

GUSSIE: You wait until papa dies and then you starve.

YETTA: My papa died on the ship.

GUSSIE: I'm sorry. I shouldn't have said anything.

YETTA: The point is that not all of us have matchmakers finding us husbands while we're at work. Some of us would like time to look at a boy in the street, maybe to be looked at by one.

GUSSIE: Maybe some of us should have stuck to the old ways.

YETTA: Maybe we should. In which case I would probably be a prostitute.

GUSSIE: A person who is a prostitute is so because that's what she is, not because of Torah or Mr. Blanck or anybody else. I could be a prostitute if I wanted.

YETTA: I'm sure you could.

GUSSIE: THAT'S NOT WHAT I MEANT!

YETTA: What did you mean?

GUSSIE: I don't even remember now, you've got me so mixed up. *(Pause)* You could meet a boy here.

YETTA: Maybe I have

GUSSIE: *(Not hearing her)* That tall boy with the yellow hair—

YETTA: The tall boy with the yellow hair.

GUSSIE: Upstairs—

YETTA: Theodore.

GUSSIE: He looks at you all the time.

YETTA: It would be nice to be looked at sometime when you're not sweaty and covered in lint. *(Pause)* All the Catholic girls have boyfriends.

GUSSIE: They do it differently. They can open their blouses a button or two. They can look at each other in the street, the boys and the girls

YETTA: The rabbis get together to see what new thing they can add to make the lives of our women more difficult.

GUSSIE: Yetta—

YETTA: If you look you can always find a verse in the Torah to grind us down a little more—

GUSSIE: Stop it! You always take it too far! *(Pause)* Yes, an open window sometimes would be nice.

YETTA: *(Smiling, a point scored. Then teasingly)* Theodore, the boy with the yellow hair that works upstairs—

GUSSIE: Yes? *(Getting it)* Oh my God, Yetta, THAT'S why he looks at you all the time?

YETTA: I never looked back until I saw him at a meeting.

GUSSIE: One of your meetings?

YETTA: Yes.

GUSSIE: That sweet boy is a Socialist?

YETTA: Yes.

GUSSIE: Do Socialists marry and raise families?

YETTA: How do you suppose we get little Socialists? We were side by side in the folding chairs one night. Theodore and me. The room wasn't crowded, but he came over and sat down by me. There was free coffee. Emma Goldman was speaking—

GUSSIE: *(Covering her ears) No!*

YETTA: What is the matter with you?

GUSSIE: Emma Goldman has lovers!

YETTA: Oh! Who knows what people mean when they say that?

GUSSIE: She has been in prison!

YETTA: Yes she has. And she made us all feel ashamed that we had not been.

GUSSIE: She's an ANARCHIST.

YETTA: Yes she is, and if you can tell me what that is I will give you five dollars right out of my petticoat. *(Silence) Anyway,* when the meeting was over we sat and talked and talked. He leaned in close, his yellow hair falling down over his eyes so he had to brush it away, and every time he did he smiled like a little boy. They closed the hall around us and we had to sneak out through the big window in back that Theodore knows that's always open. Oh, the words he has! He's going to the university—

GUSSIE: A Jew?

YETTA: Yes, a Jew. This isn't Russia. His father is a rabbi.

GUSSIE: Oh! You're going to be a *rabbitzin*!

YETTA: Hush! It's no such thing. He hasn't asked me yet. The word "marriage" hasn't been said. There have been...two or three nights...nights like honey...talking...holding hands because we were so enthralled with the cause we didn't notice...we felt such sympathy with each other, with the workers. We burn with such pity for the people, the same compassion aflame in two hearts. Besides, he's not going to be a rabbi.

GUSSIE: But, if his father—

YETTA: Again, this isn't Russia.

GUSSIE: But to throw away such a life!

YETTA: Theodore feels it wouldn't be right. He's lost his faith.

GUSSIE: He's no longer a Jew?

YETTA: Well—

GUSSIE: You can't not be a Jew once you are one.

YETTA: Of course he's a Jew, but—

GUSSIE: A Jew and not a Jew. That sounds like one of those musicals down at the Peoples' Theater.

YETTA: Which you never go to.

GUSSIE: Which I never go to. But that doesn't mean I can't look at the posters and shake my head sadly at the ruination of the world. Is he a Jew or isn't he?

YETTA: He's a Jew who doesn't believe in God.

GUSSIE: And I'm a tiger who has decided to eat no more meat.

YETTA: Making it ridiculous doesn't make it wrong. It's a different world from the world of our fathers. Everything is farther away. Everything is a journey. You want to believe what they told you in the cradle, but you can't anymore. How much faith would Abraham have had if God hadn't been there all the time, rousing him from sleep with something new to do?

GUSSIE: I'm a rabbi that I should know this?

YETTA: You have a brain. Tell me the last time God spoke to you. Tell me the last time you saw His hand at work in your life.

GUSSIE: We're Christians now that God has to talk to us all of the time? Why do we have the Torah? Why do we have the rabbis?

YETTA: It's a good thing you're pretty. It would not be such a *tsoriss* if we had a better life.

GUSSIE: No it would not. You go shopping for it in one street, I in another, this better life. We don't have to quarrel all the time.

YETTA: We weren't quarreling! We were— *(Catching her own tone)* Oh. I do sound like I'm quarreling, don't I?

GUSSIE: You get used to it. Sometimes I don't even notice. Where are those lazy girls? It's nearly five o' clock

YETTA: We spoil them.

GUSSIE: They know we'll get things started.

YETTA: Avi gets us started.

GUSSIE: Maybe God whispers in Avi's ear just like Abraham. "Get up Avi! Pick up a broom that I will show you!"

They share a chuckle.

YETTA: I used to hate threading the needles.

GUSSIE: You forget what you hate after a while.

YETTA: Then you forget what you love.

GUSSIE: *(Real distress)* Oh, Yetta, you want your children to be fathered by a man who has no God?

YETTA: You wouldn't let that pass, would you? First, I don't have children. Second, if I did, I'd want them to be fathered by a man who believes what he believes, not what other people have told him for a hundred years. *(Pause)* You have nothing to say?

GUSSIE: Nothing I won't regret. *(Pause, working)* I have not lost my faith.

YETTA: I expect not.

GUSSIE: I'm grateful to God for all his handiwork. Kings of the earth, and all peoples, let them praise the name of the Lord!

YETTA: I didn't say I had lost my faith, Gussie, I said Theodore has.

GUSSIE: A man and a woman are one flesh.

YETTA: Oh dear—

GUSSIE: I thank God that my parents are alive to guide me. I thank God for the Torah.

YETTA: As well you should.

GUSSIE: I thank God for work.

YETTA: *THIS* work?

GUSSIE: Especially this work. At the end of the day we're too exhausted to argue about anything.

YETTA: And I go home worried that I've hurt your feelings.

GUSSIE: Good.

> *Just then, a bit of a music hall tune is sung in the hall. ESSIE enters as sunny as the conversation has become serious. Essie sports some ornament or article of clothing that sets her off from the other two.*

GUSSIE: A *maidel mit* a *klaidel*...

YETTA: *(Of the ornament)* You better put that away before Mrs. Panno sees it.

GUSSIE: She'll think they're paying you too much.

YETTA: She'll accuse you of stealing it. You didn't steal it, did you?

ESSIE: *(Curtseying) Bonjour.*

GUSSIE & YETTA: *Guten Morgan,* Essie.

ESSIE: I could hear you bickering clear down the corridor.

GUSSIE: We are Solomon and Daniel solving the world's problems.

ESSIE: Well, today I don't need you, because I have no problems at all! *(Looking about)* It's always so clean in the morning!

GUSSIE: Elves.

ESSIE: I thought it was you. You're always here when I get here.

GUSSIE: So you noticed?

ESSIE: Get those few more pieces done to attract Mr. Blanck's eye—

YETTA: If we did a hootchy-cootch down on Greene Street it wouldn't attract Mr. Blanck's eye.

GUSSIE: Oh yes it would—

YETTA: Well, yes it would, but, to finish my thought, we come early because if we left most of you to thread the needles we'd spend the whole morning untangling and starting again.

ESSIE: Most of *us*?

YETTA: The new girls. The beginners.

ESSIE: And we do so appreciate it. Not all of us want our hands looking like we hauled in nets all day.

GUSSIE: *(Fingering the special item of Essie's clothing)* This is store-bought!

ESSIE: This isn't Poland. We're allowed to go to the store.

GUSSIE: Oh, so you found a store where they won't take money—

YETTA: Where they give you things according to your good looks—

ESSIE: That's exactly it. They took one look and gave me boxes and boxes—

YETTA: You're breezy as a March morning. Did you finally get a kiss from what's-his-name the grocer?

ESSIE: Reuben. And no, it was better than that.

They stare at her. She begins humming a theater tune.

YETTA: You've been to the theater!

GUSSIE: *(Beside herself)* Oh! Was it Thomashevsky?

ESSIE: No—

GUSSIE: He's so handsome!

ESSIE: He's in London playing for the king. Something. We went uptown. That's why I had to have this! You can't walk into the music hall wearing the same thing you wore to work. You can't walk in there wearing something your mama pieced together for you.

GUSSIE: Who? Who'd you see?
   (Essie begins sashaying around like a red-hot mama, la-laing a vaudeville tune)
Can you guess?

YETTA: Sophie Tucker!

GUSSIE: She is very shameful!

ESSIE: Oh, that is the one thing she is not—

YETTA: How much can you remember?

ESSIE: I remember everything!
   (While the others continue working, Essie gets herself in position, delivers a Tuckeresque rendering of)
Some of these days
You'll miss your honey
Some of these days
You'll feel so lonely

You'll miss my hugging
You'll miss my kisses
You'll miss me, honey
When you go away

I feel so lonely
Just for you only
For you know, honey
You've had your way

And when you leave me
I know you'll grieve me
You'll miss your little honey
Some of these days

   Applause. Essie bows dramatically.

YETTA: You must love the shirtwaist factory; otherwise, your name would be up in lights! Think of the dresses you could wear, twirling around with your shoes showing!

ESSIE: I did. All night long.

GUSSIE: That's a sad song for the music hall.

ESSIE: Oh, they bring you down, they boost you up. The women in the theater all wear beautiful gowns. Furs and lace and layers of…I don't know what. Somebody makes them. While we're piecing together waists for working girls, somebody is embroidering tulle and satin and cashmere. Somebody sews pearls onto silken threads and dangles them from bodices. Reuben says that could be us. If we wanted he could set us up in a little shop. We could—

GUSSIE: It's enough that you believe Reuben's stories. They won't get him a kiss from us.

YETTA: There aren't enough crates of cabbage in New York to buy such a place—

ESSIE: Well, one day when I'm missing from Panno's roll call—

Din is heard in the hall. The ITALIAN GIRLS are coming. They breeze through the door, crossing themselves as they come.

YETTA: *Besser spate wie niemals!*

GUSSIE: They're always crossing themselves.

YETTA: There's so many Jews here. They're afraid they'll burst into flame.

Essie salutes the girls as they walk in.

ESSIE: Rosaria! Lucia! *(Aside, to Yetta)* Rosaria is here. Start the countdown. I've got twenty.

YETTA: I've got twenty-five. One...two...

GUSSIE: Eighteen—

The new girls flurry about putting their things away and setting their work spaces in order as Yetta continues counting.

YETTA: Three...four...
(*Rosaria walks back toward the door, which she eyes expectantly*)
five...six...seven...

ESSIE: Do you see him?

ROSARIA: Not yet.

LUCIA: Does anybody have ten?

YETTA: You do now. Eight...nine...ten...
(*Lucia shrugs off defeat*)
eleven...twelve...

Before Yetta says 'thirteen,' Avi launches through the door.

GUSSIE: *(Triumphant)* I win! Not a record, but still a good showing—

However precipitous he was at the door, Avi is now all bashful and hat-in-hand. He approaches Rosaria with excruciating courtesy. He has a flower in his hand.

ESSIE: You were a laggard in love today, Avi.

AVI: What do you mean?

ESSIE: Usually she doesn't even get through the door—

AVI: *(To Rosaria, oblivious)* Bella signorina—

ROSARIA: Shalom, Mar Nussbaum—

> Both clumps of girls turn away and giggle. Avi and Rosaria are oblivious. He gives the flower and she weaves it into her hair. They move close together. They clasp hands, staring ardently into each other's eyes. The girls can hardly contain themselves.

AVI: Um...I'm glad to see you today. *Mi piace*...see you...*videre?* Uh—

LUCIA: *Oggi.*

AVI: *Oggi.*

ESSIE: Oh, look at the face on that boy! Avi, you don't need to say anything at all.

GUSSIE: They start so young now. Makes me feel like an old maid.

YETTA: Two months without... Three months without... Then it's a year, then it's a lifetime—

GUSSIE: You shut up.

AVI: *Io ti amoro.* *(To Lucia)* Is that anything like it?
   (Lucia shrugs and nods: yes and no)
Well, I guess I'd better get back to work. *Io lavoro!* Mrs. Panno is here already. You know how she appears out of the walls. See you afterwards. *Si?* I'll walk you home. *(Makes a sign in the air, two sets of fingers walking home)*

ROSARIA: *Si. Ciao, mio bello.*

Avi departs with many a backward glance. Pause.

ESSIE: Are you going to tell him your English is perfectly good?

ROSARIA: Why? You see how pretty he is when he's trying so hard.

GUSSIE: You must be the reason his yarmulke is wadded up in his pocket when he goes out onto the Square.

LUCIA: It's a new age, Gussie.

GUSSIE: So everyone is telling me. You'd think there'd be a nice Jewish girl—

LUCIA: You'd think there'd be a nice Italian boy—

GUSSIE: My Uncle Shlomo says he knew somebody who once dated a Moor.

YETTA: Of course the Moor was a Jew.

ESSIE: The pope wears a yarmulke. I've seen pictures.

GUSSIE: Of course he does. Do you think *he'd* go out on the street with his head uncovered?

ROSARIA: It's to remind everyone that Jesus was a Jew.

LUCIA: He was not!

ROSARIA: Before he was the Savior, yes he was.

LUCIA: Rosie, don't even say things like that!

ROSARIA: Until he went to Rome and became a Catholic, yes he was. The monsignor has a picture book that says—

GUSSIE: Wait. Where's Albina?

Silence.

YETTA: WHERE IS ALBINA?

LUCIA: If you say it loud enough maybe Panno will hear.

ROSARIA: She is sick today.

ESSIE: Sick? She can't be sick. Not again. Panno will have her fired—

ROSARIA: She can't get the medicine. She can't recover until—

GUSSIE: She and her four babies? She can't—

> *Noise without. Gussie utters a muffled sound. They look at her. She's frozen, except for her hands which are frantically waving them to their work stations. Thither they run and begin working their machines. Mrs. Panno strides magisterially in. She is a large, formidable woman, older than the others, with authority bestowed on her by the owners of the factory. She hopes to catch lollygagging. In this, for the moment, she is disappointed. She strides slowly around the room, touching this, inspecting that, sniffing and peering, while the girls keep their eyes down and concentrate on their sewing.*

MRS. PANNO: Any problems?

> *This is addressed to Yetta, but Yetta pointedly does not answer. There is an uncomfortable silence until Rosaria finally pipes up.*

ROSARIA: No problems, Mrs. Panno.

MRS. PANNO: *(Counting with her eyes)* Where is that Caruso girl?

LUCIA: Albina?

MRS. PANNO: Yes, Albina. If she can't be trusted to come to work—

ROSARIA: Oh, she's just—

MRS. PANNO: She had a cough—

LUCIA: Everyone has a cough.

YETTA: Albina is downstairs in the store room. Getting—

GUSSIE: More thread—

YETTA: Getting more thread.

MRS. PANNO: There's plenty of thread.

LUCIA: It was so damp from the rain last night. We thought we'd get some that was dry—

YETTA: —so that our work need never be interrupted.

MRS. PANNO: *(Pause. Panno harumphs. Then)* Some of the machines are threaded wrong.

YETTA: They're not wrong.

MRS. PANNO: They're not the way it's done here.

YETTA: If you actually ever used the machines—

ROSARIA: We'll get right on it, Mrs. Panno.

Panno strides up very close to Yetta, trying to be menacing.

MRS. PANNO: Goldstein?

YETTA: Panno?
(Mrs. Panno gives up, strides out, taking time to glare at Yetta, who pretends not to notice. When Panno is out of sight)
Klafte.

ROSARIA: I don't know why she hasn't fired you yet.

YETTA: Because she can't. Only the bosses can do that. She's a tool of the bosses but she's not a boss.

ESSIE: That's worse, isn't it?

YETTA: Yes, it is worse.

ESSIE: All the dirty looks and none of the fun.

GUSSIE: I think it's because she has a tender heart.

YETTA: Oh, please—

GUSSIE: She has to be all hard in front of the bosses, but really—

LUCIA: My cousin Tritta knows her. She says she goes to the opera by herself and cries and cries—

GUSSIE: All you people cry at the opera. It doesn't mean—

YETTA: The Czar cries at the opera—

GUSSIE: But she understands how hard it is to—

YETTA: That's worse still. A robber with a tender heart. I hate to think—

ESSIE: Yetta hates to have her world view blurred by subtleties—

GUSSIE: Anyway, what good is it to push her too far?

ESSIE: It's like poking a bear with a stick—

GUSSIE: She could go and tattle to Mr. Blanck and Mr. Harris, God forbid, and get us all fired for harboring a—whatever it is that you are, Yetta.

LUCIA: A suffragette.

ESSIE: An anarchist.

GUSSIE: See! They'll think you've corrupted us with...some corruption you can't even name. Is that what you want, Yetta Goldstein? For us all to be tossed into the street?

LUCIA: They won't do that. Who would make the shirtwaists?

ESSIE: *Oy!* You opened the door—

YETTA: On hiring day there's a line clear across Washington Square. We're in here slaving away so we don't see. Girls in white blouses and blue skirts just like us, by the dozens, by the twenties, longing for a job, any job. Girls right off the boats. Girls just turned fourteen and expected to carry their own weight. We make less than we did two years ago because they know they can fire one of us and hire ten desperate girls from the street. The colored girls won't even come here. They're too ashamed. They've done slavery once and they know it now when they see it.

GUSSIE: I'd like to know when it's been different.

YETTA: Am I a scholar that I should know that? But I do know that whatever happened in the past, it could be different in the future. If we stopped work. Shut off the machines. If we went on strike. If we locked the doors—

ROSARIA: The doors are already locked—

YETTA: Yes, they are locked because the bosses locked them. WE must lock them. We lock them from the inside and show that it is our factory—our labor, our grit and sweat, and we'll let the bosses in when we find something useful for them to do. We struck once. It wasn't a success, but it wasn't a disaster, either. We could try again, knowing what we know now—

Pause.

GUSSIE: I think somebody has been going to too many meetings.

ROSARIA: Oh! I broke my thread!

Yetta gets up to change Rosaria's thread.

YETTA: The prophet Nathan rebuked King David for taking away Uriah's one possession, his beautiful wife, when he himself had so much. How many boys are without their wives because we are closed up in here, because we are gathered into the treasury of those who already have so much?

GUSSIE: It's shameful for a woman to quote scripture.

YETTA: *(Exhausted, crestfallen)* The system would never defeat me, Gussie, but you can. With a single sentence. You ought to go into politics, *(To Rosaria)* There, that ought to work. You're pulling too hard.

ROSARIA: Trying to make the day go faster—

LUCIA: We could play a game.

YETTA: The initials game!

GUSSIE: Yes!

ESSIE: Oh, I have one! I'm thinking of the most wonderful man in the universe and his initial are—

ALL: REUBEN THE GROCER.

Silence. All bend to their work Then Lucia utters a pained sound, bends over at her machine a little.

ROSARIA: Lucitta, what is it?

LUCIA: Nothing. *(Again)* OH!

YETTA: Lucia!

LUCIA: I don't feel well.

Yetta gets up and looks out the door.

YETTA: Panno is gone for the moment. If you need to use the bathroom, you can. Just don't take too long.

LUCIA: The last time the door was locked.

YETTA: Then go on the floor. That will teach them a lesson.

Lucia exits.

GUSSIE: —and now we know why the corridor stinks—

ESSIE: It's the heat.

ROSARIA: It's not the heat.
(Steady stares at her)
She's my sister. I promised I wouldn't tell! She'll pull my hair out by the roots—

ESSIE: Oh, dear God.

GUSSIE: What? What? "Oh, dear God" what?

ESSIE: Is she?
(Silence)
IS she?

Rosaria nods.

GUSSIE: Everyone in the world knows what's going on except me. *(Getting it)* Oh!

GUSSIE: Is she married?

ROSARIA: A shame it is on you to ask that!

YETTA: A woman *can* get pregnant without being married you know.

ESSIE: Maybe she can and maybe she can't but of course our Lucia is married. *(Not so confident, to Rosaria)* Isn't she?

ROSARIA: Yes, dear Christ, this year and a half. You think every Catholic girl is a *puttana*.

ESSIE: I might think that if I knew what it was.

ROSARIA: Well, she isn't one, so don't worry about it.

ESSIE: There's no ring.

GUSSIE: Catholics are different. We shouldn't judge.

ROSARIA: Who can afford a ring? Besides, the misters don't like married women. They get sick. They have babies. They miss days. They think about their husbands.

GUSSIE: She could have told us. Aren't we family?

YETTA: Family or not we have big flapping jaws, and one of us would say something that would come to Panno's ears, and she would run to the bosses like the good spaniel she is and then Lucia could be fired with a baby coming and her husband breaking his back on the docks for a few pennies a day.

ROSARIA: It's more than that—

YETTA: THE POINT IS—we keep Lucia's secret as long as we can. Babies have been born here in this room and the mothers didn't need to lose a day's pay. Before us there was a little girl over in the Diamond Shirtwaist Factory that was born there and nursed there and her diapers were scraps out of the scrap bin and it was her home until the day she applied for a job herself. It's all in the keeping silent. They don't *want* to know. They want us to keep our lives secret so they don't have to think about us.

ESSIE: *(Wickedly)* Oh! Maybe it was Panno!

They laugh.

GUSSIE: She did come over from the Diamond when it burned.

ROSARIA: So maybe it was her!

GUSSIE: Mr. Blanck and Mr. Harris owned that one, too, and one night they burned it for the insurance money.

YETTA: You listen to too many stories, Gussie.

ROSARIA: Is that legal?

YETTA: If you're rich it is.

ESSIE: Was anybody—

GUSSIE: No. They had the decency to wait till late at night.

ESSIE: Doesn't seem like them to take so much care.

GUSSIE: That was a while ago. You get old, you get mean. Look at Yetta there.

Yetta sticks out her tongue. Lucia re-enters.

LUCIA: Well, that's better. *(Pause)* Breakfast was not setting well.

GUSSIE: My sister Esther started getting morning sickness on the very day—
(Lucia lets out a screech. She assesses the situation, and knows to blame her sister. She turns in fury upon her sister, boxing her ears)
You told! *Una brutta! Una stregga!* (Etc., ad lib)

ROSARIA: *(Fleeing for her life)* It was going to come out anyway. It just slipped, I swear to Jesus—

LUCIA: The knife I put into your back won't come out so easy. *Brutta testa di merda! (Etc., ad lib)*

Sudden noise in the hall. They freeze in place.

ROSARIA: *(sotto voce)* Panno?

YETTA: Shhh!

ESSIE: Panno is usually quieter than that—

Avi enters.

LUCIA: You scared us to death!

He's pushing a broom, cleaning up whatever mess might have been made since his last go-through. It looks like he's ignoring Rosaria.

AVI: I come with glad tidings.

YETTA: I'll just bet.

AVI: Party on the roof this afternoon!

LUCIA: For us?
(All roll their eyes in unison)
I'm so hungry. When you said "party" I thought of tangerine sherbets, almond biscotti and cinnamon dates and *crema di mascarponi* and shellfish open on the linguine and—

YETTA: Will you stop!

GUSSIE: I don't know what any of that is and my mouth is watering.

YETTA: Avi, if you can't stop torturing us then just go away.

AVI: I'll come down to get you. All you have to do is smile. Try to be pleasant, Yetta. Five minutes at most. Say, don't you want to hear what I learned this morning? *Gennario. Fabrio. Marzo, Aprille, Maggio…*
(The Italian girls applaud. He holds his hand up to tell them "Wait." He does his sing-song routine)
GennNArio, FABrio, MarzoAPrilMAggiO…

They shrug. He smiles and begins to sing, and when he does he brings it right to Rosaria.

AVI: *(Sings, low but sweet)*
Precious prize, close your eyes,
Now we're goin' to visit love's paradise,
Press your lips again to mine,
Love is king of ev'ry thing,

Squeeze me dear, I don't care!
Hug me just as if you were a grizzly bear,
This is how I'll go through life,
No care or strife, when you're my wife.

Rosaria begins to complete the pop hit of the day, and then everybody joins in. They do not all know the lyrics equally well.

ROSARIA, THEN ALL:
Oh! you beautiful doll,
You great big beautiful doll!
Let me put my arms about you,
I could never live without you;

Oh! you beautiful doll,
You great big beautiful doll!
If you ever leave me how my heart will ache,
I want to hug you but I fear you'd break.
Oh, oh, oh, oh,
Oh, you beautiful doll!

> *They laugh. Avi kisses Rosaria's hand and leaves. Then they sit quietly, sobering up, their hands still busy at the machines. One of them sighs.*

LUCIA: A party!

YETTA: It's not for us.

GUSSIE: I have no idea how I know that song.

SCENE TWO

On the roof the Triangle Building, a festive table is set out. Avi staggers on under the weight of a box of cake, plates, a jug of punch, party favors, etc., clearly intended for a children's party. He may need to make more than one trip. He interrupts his labors to go to the edge of the building, lean over, and take in the city.

AVI: *(Of the city below)* A *mehaya*.
   (Mrs. Panno enters behind him)
Oh! I'm glad you're here. I wouldn't know how to set anything on the table right.

MRS. PANNO: Fork here. Napkin there. It's nothing.

AVI: Mother tries to teach you, but—

MRS. PANNO: It's for the girls. Men sit down and they eat. What do they have to know? I'm sure there's more to come up.

AVI: I know. I'll go soon. I live in the basement. I want to look at the city from here. Just for a minute. Isn't it beautiful?

MRS. PANNO: Yes it is.

AVI: Oh! There's the arch, and the park—

MRS. PANNO: You can see the neighborhood where I grew up if you look over there.

AVI: Whatever you can't see from here doesn't need to be seen. Look! The pigeons are flying UNDER us! *(Flapping his shirt to get cool)* There is so much *air*. You forget. Why are all the doors locked?

MRS. PANNO: So the girls don't do what you're doing.

AVI: Breathing?

MRS. PANNO: Lollygagging.

AVI: A glimpse of the sky every once in a while can't hurt. Back in Austria my grandfather gave his workers treats to encourage them to work harder. Licorice. Cold cider. An hour to sit under a tree.

MRS. PANNO: That was Austria. That was your grandfather.

AVI: It must be hard for a tyrant to decide whether he'd rather have efficiency or obedience.

MRS. PANNO: What?

AVI: Nothing. *(Mischievously)* I was just wondering if you could help me with my Italian.

MRS. PANNO: You could help yourself with your employment by bringing the rest of the decorations up. The children will be here in an hour.
   (He turns to go back for more party stuff. She pauses)
Avi?

AVI: Yes?

MRS. PANNO: All right. You can stay up here until the children come. Just don't tattle on me.

AVI: Never.

MRS. PANNO: It does seem free up here. Wide and free. You can get to the other roofs if you're a good jumper. *(Exits)*

AVI: How in the world do you know that? *(Avi tours the roof, beside himself with the sudden freedom. He may run from one side to the other)* I could. I could jump that easy. One roof to the other clear down to the shore, and then I'd take my clothes off and jump in and be cool and clean. I forget whether you can swim to Austria or not. Maybe the bosses will let Rosaria and me get married up here. The girls will make her gown. We'll release a cage of white pigeons. We'll have a priest and a rabbi and my sisters won't stop crying. *(He looks around to insure he is alone, then begins to sing* "Du Bist Dos Likht Fun Mayne Oyg'n" *from an old Second Avenue musical, words and music available in* The New York Times' Great Songs of the Yiddish Theater. *He has seen the show and has the performer's motions down pat. Sings)*
Oy, mayn tayer Yosele
Du bist gut un fayn
Azoy flegt zingen Reyzele
Mir in oyer arayn
Ven ikh fil dikh lebn mir
Git mayn harts a pik
Du host mayn harts gegebn mir
Nem es nit tsurik
Leben ken ikh nit on dir
Zoltsu visn zayn
Veystu vos du meynst tsu mir
Yosl, her zikh ayn:

Du bist dos likht fun mayne oygn
Nor du bashaynst mayn velt far mir
Du host mikh tsu zikh tsugetsoygn
Az lebn ken ikh on dir.
Du makhst mayn nakht zol likhtik vern
Dem bloyen himl brengstu mir.

Du bist mayn heler morgnshtern
Nu shayn far mir ikh bet bay dir

Bistu nit lebnmir
Iz mir khoyshekh finyster,
Un derher ikh dayn shtim
Vert tog in ayedn vinkt
Du bist dos likht fun mayne oygn
Nor du bashaynst mayn velt far mir

MRS. PANNO: *(Bellows from offstage)* Avi!

> *Avi nearly jumps out of his skin, runs for more party stuff. Panno returns to the roof. She rather tenderly continues to lay the stuff out for the children's party.*

SCENE THREE

On the roof. The sound of children playing at some distance, as though the party had receded to another part. Essie is huddled at the very edge. She looks uncomfortable and like she is trying to conceal herself. After a few beats, a bright rubber ball bounces onto the stage, pursued by a merry Avi, who runs unexpectedly into Essie.

AVI: Essie!

ESSIE: Oh, Avi, you won't—

AVI: Won't what?

ESSIE: Tell on me.

Avi turns and throws the ball back toward the sound of playing.

AVI: Not unless you were going to throw yourself off the roof. Then I might tell somebody. What are you doing?

ESSIE: I'm hiding.

AVI: You're not liking the party?

ESSIE: *Please.*

AVI: You can have fun almost anywhere if you set your mind to it.

ESSIE: After the night I had I can't even pretend to be content with this.

AVI: I missed the morning gossip. You and Reuben?

ESSIE: Me and Reuben and Sophie Tucker.

AVI: I played ball with some boys in the Square until it was dark. They can all do Sophie Tucker, with her hands on their hips and her big bosoms shaking. The boys put balls down their shirts and wiggle. Six or seven of us at once is quite a sight.

ESSIE: I heard you laughing just now, traitor.

AVI: I was having fun.

ESSIE: I wish I could. The children love you.

AVI: Oh, I just know a few games—

ESSIE: You're practically their age. They don't even know you're—

AVI: I'm what?

ESSIE: An employee.

AVI: Thanks for the reminder. I was content for about fifteen minutes.

ESSIE: Sorry.

AVI: Usually it's Yetta who says stuff like that.

ESSIE: Sorry.

AVI: Essie—?

ESSIE: What?

AVI: There's something the matter. You look frightened. I won't tell on you—

ESSIE: Oh, not that—

AVI: The kids? They're monsters but they're not that bad—

ESSIE: I... It's not the children. It's not just the children. There's something on the roof. It was—disturbing. There was something on the roof when I looked over.

AVI: What do you mean?

ESSIE: *(Pointing)* Over there. It was on this roof, but when it saw me it...it disappeared. Then it was there. Oh, Avi, it's a ghost!

AVI: A ghost?
  (Essie nods emphatically. Avi goes to the very edge and peers)
That?

ESSIE: Don't make me look! It's a ghost. It wailed at me, and then there was a flutter of white and—

AVI: Essie, it's a bird. *Ein Nachtschwarmer.* I don't know what they call it here. Nighthawk, I guess. *Nachtschwarmer.* It's just a bird.

ESSIE: No...no...it changed. For a moment it was one thing, then it was another...a terrible cry, and then it just lifted up—

AVI: You frightened it. We had them at home. I guess they're the same here. They don't build a nest, but lay their eggs wherever they can find a space. Out in the open. On ledges, on the flat of roofs. It's not very safe, but it's what they have. They're like us. No place for our nests. Shut out from the day, having to take wing in darkness, having to pick up the leftovers; still, here we are, on the top of the world, looking down on everybody. Scaring everybody who thinks we must be ghosts.

ESSIE: A nighthawk.

AVI: I think so.

ESSIE: I thought pigeons were the only birds in the city.

AVI: Nope.

ESSIE: Wild things, even here. I never thought—

AVI: Above us and below us, creeping across our windowsills when we're asleep. It's best that we don't know about them. It's best that we don't know about a whole lot of things. The *Nachtschwarmers* are all right, though. They're always there if you know where to look. You hear their calls above you at first of night. It's like they're guardian spirits, watching over. You should listen.

ESSIE: I'll listen. Tonight I'll listen. I feel foolish now.

AVI: Better than what you'd feel if it really was a ghost.

ESSIE: Nighthawk. So of course it looks out of place in the day.

AVI: Of course. Out of place. After we leave work it spreads its wings and sails out hunting over Washington Square. It's the night shift. When we return it's already asleep.

ESSIE: We never see each other.

AVI: I bet Panno does. I bet they see each other. She's here before me, and I think she lingers after, though I've never stayed around to see.

ESSIE: Panno and the nighthawks.

AVI: Yes. Making sure everything is all right. Guarding the evening and the morning.

ESSIE: Maybe she IS a nighthawk.

AVI: A shapeshifter. Maybe. That would explain some things—

ESSIE: Have you ever seen a ghost?

AVI: Have you ever seen Panno creeping around the machines at dawn? That's all the haunting I need. Are you going to smile now that there's no ghost?

ESSIE: There's something worse.

AVI: What?

ESSIE: When I came over here and saw the ghost, I was trying to get away from something else. Something worse.

AVI: WHAT?

ESSIE: The children—

AVI: The— Here on the roof?

ESSIE: Yes.

AVI: They're not ghosts either.

ESSIE: It's not that. I just— It's just that—

AVI: What?

ESSIE: You won't be disgusted with me?

AVI: How would I know until you tell me?

ESSIE: I hate them. I hate the children. I hate them and I don't want to.

AVI: They're too young to—

ESSIE: I know everything you're going to say, so don't bother. It's not politics. I'm not Yetta. It's—what if I hate all children, Avi, not just the ones I have an excuse to? I think I hate them because they're Mr. Blanck's, but what if I just hate children, all of them, even my own, God forbid? What if I hate Reuben's children when the time comes? What if I hate them from a greedy dark soul? What if I'm so selfish I want all of Reuben's attention and never want a child in my arms coming between us? I want jewelry and clothes and every penny spent on a baby drives me wild with jealousy—what if it's that?

AVI: I don't think there's any such person as that, Essie. I think you're all right. I think right feelings come when they're needed. I hate them too when I allow myself to think about their fine clothes and the inches of icing on their little cakes. I picture myself tossing the ball and it flying over the side and they one by one gliding off to fetch it like so many puppies, off into the air and then hitting the ground with a little cake-y splat. But then I think it's not their fault how they're born, and we're playmates again. And then I love them. Really. I'm glad to love them. Maybe they'll remember me... And show kindness... To someone...

ESSIE: But I do really hate them.

AVI: I know.

ESSIE: And I have to pretend—

AVI: I know. But you're good at that, aren't you?

She gives him a playful swat.

ESSIE: I have no idea how I'm going to get down off this roof. I've been hiding so long—

AVI: I'm going to run out and you're going to follow me. We'll go back to the party. We'll be shouting and laughing and carrying on, and they'll think we were having a good time over here by ourselves, and Mrs. Blanck will smile on us because our good time was because of her lovely children and everything will be all right, and the nighthawks will come back and rest themselves until dusk and then they'll watch over us as we trudge home and nobody will be the wiser.

ESSIE: What if Rosaria sees us?

AVI: Maybe she'll be *ein bischen* jealous. Maybe then I won't have to work so hard.

ESSIE: You're worse than I am.

AVI: Oh, much, much worse.

They do as Avi suggested.

SCENE FOUR

Workroom, several hours later. The workroom stands empty, except for Mrs. Panno, who is poking into the girls' personal belongings. Yetta appears silently in the doorway, watching her. Finally Panno notices Yetta with a start.

MRS. PANNO: Oh! You nearly gave me— What are you doing here?

YETTA: I work here.

MRS. PANNO: You were summoned upstairs.

YETTA: I went. And now I'm back.

MRS. PANNO: Were you dismissed?

YETTA: I didn't say I was dismissed.

MRS. PANNO: You can't just be walking around on your own—

YETTA: Clearly I can—

MRS. PANNO: What I mean is—

YETTA: What DO you mean, Mrs. Panno?

MRS. PANNO: Mrs. Blanck was hoping—

YETTA: If our employer wanted us to do something else he should be paying us to do something else. Do we get paid for the time we're away from our machines?

MRS. PANNO: Of course not.

YETTA: Can we estimate the number of waists we would have assembled, and get paid for them?

MRS. PANNO: That's ridiculous.

YETTA: Is it? If we're being paid for our time, then the bosses should pay us for the time we spend doing what they want, whatever it happens to be. If we're being paid by the piece, then they should not take us away from our piecework.

MRS. PANNO: Didn't you get cake?

YETTA: The cake was for the children. We got to watch them cut it.

MRS. PANNO: I can't wait until someone gives you a factory and you can run it just the way you want. *(Getting no response)* Where is that Caruso woman? If I find she's been absent—

YETTA: She went up on the roof with everyone else, as commanded. It's not her fault if you didn't notice her. Maybe she scurried downstairs to get a little work done.

MRS. PANNO: *(With elaborate patience)* Mr. Blanck's family is visiting for the day. He just wanted everyone to meet the children. So we can be a big...family, all of us. That doesn't seem such a horrible thing, does it?

YETTA: No—

MRS. PANNO: Avi was like one of them. He loved the children.

YETTA: He is one of them.

MRS. PANNO: He didn't pull a long face and lament his lost pennies.

YETTA: Not out loud.

MRS. PANNO: The other girls seemed so happy, cooing at the children, all smiling and—

YETTA: It's hard to imagine what other response the girls could allow themselves. I'm not blaming the children, but we were not invited upstairs to meet them. We were summoned so that the children might review their property, so that they might watch us bowing and nattering and pasting smiles on our faces so they can remember how slaves should behave to their masters. All so that they might recognize us in the future and put us to good use.

MRS. PANNO: If you don't like things as they are, maybe you should get out.

YETTA: If you don't like things as they will be, maybe *you* should get out.

MRS. PANNO: Nobody here is a slave.

YETTA: For nine hours a day, yes we are. Even you, though you can't admit it. Why are you stealing from us?

MRS. PANNO: What?

YETTA: *(Mocking) What?* I saw you when I came back. I SAW you. Your hands in our purses and the pockets of our coats.

MRS. PANNO: I was not stealing from you! I won't have you saying that! You are not allowed to say that!

YETTA: Thief.

MRS. PANNO: Stop it!

YETTA: You and the bosses are in league. You're a gang. Just like the Irish boys in the Bowery. If we fall within your power we are lost. You summon us to a meeting, then dock our pay because we're not in our work places, and while we have to pretend to adore the little masters, you creep down to steal from us. Shame! Don't you answer back to me! Shame!

Angrily, Panno empties her pockets and slams the contents of one (maybe a handkerchief and a lorgnette) onto a table.

MRS. PANNO: There! That's how much I was stealing. Yes, Mr. Harris and Mr. Blanck sent me here, but it was to discover who is stealing from them. They know it's someone. It's always someone. They just don't know who.

YETTA: Did you find anything?

Out of the other pocket, Panno pulls the frill that Essie had sported from her night on the town.

MRS. PANNO: Just this.

YETTA: And you assume—

MRS. PANNO: No one here can afford anything like this—

YETTA: Considering what they pay us—

MRS. PANNO: Considering what you're worth—

YETTA: And where in this building has that come from?

MRS. PANNO: It doesn't matter this building. Stealing is stealing.

YETTA: Yes, Providenza, stealing is stealing. You'll take that home and make it your own and if the true owner of it protests you'll have her fired for being a thief and it doesn't matter that nothing can be proved, and nobody upstairs will care that YOU are the thief and they are your accomplices, because it is right for the rich to take and the poor to lose, and that injustice trickles down even to skulking vipers like yourself.

MRS. PANNO: I was just—

YETTA: You were just assuming nobody would call you on it. I happen to know that was bought for Essie by an admirer who took her to the theater last night, where she saw Sophie Tucker. It is hers. It is not yours. You will place it back where you found it, or I will walk down onto the street and summon a policeman.

MRS. PANNO: You'll lose your job.
(With quick and grim determination Yetta makes for the door. Panno grabs her by the arm)
Wait! There's no need for that. I made a mistake.
(She puts it back into Essie's coat. Yetta is holding the place on her arm where Panno grabbed her)
So, even my touch is poisonous now? You know I used to work at these machines just like you, years and years ago.

YETTA: Maybe you shouldn't have forgotten that.

MRS. PANNO: I have not forgotten. There is pilfering going on. You know there is.

YETTA: We know there is because you say there is. It takes twice as long for us to get out of this hellhole at night because the front exit is forbidden. We all must go around to the back and have our purses and our pockets checked, in case we have come away with an inch of lace of a spool of thread.

MRS. PANNO: An inch of lace or a spool of thread is still stealing.

YETTA: Poor Mr. Blanck. Poor Mr. Harris! They'd go bankrupt if a length of lawn went missing—

MRS. PANNO: It doesn't matter what it is or how little it's needed. Theft is—

YETTA: What would I find if I went back upstairs and went through Mrs. Blanck's purse? A bracelet bought with the hours we worked overtime and were not paid? Some pretty earrings that would have kept a girl's baby from being born too soon and too small? Slippers traded for the shoe leather we spent on sixteen flights of stairs because they couldn't be bothered to fix the elevator for an entire year? A piece of chocolate wrapped in gold paper that was all the lunches we could not afford to eat? When we burn to death behind all the doors kept locked to keep us from sneaking a cigarette or a breath of air, how will we get paid for that? Why is one stealing and the other not?

MRS. PANNO: You go to too many meetings.

YETTA: That is probably true.

MRS. PANNO: If you go to a meeting ranting and shouting all night and come to work tired and dissatisfied, you can't concentrate in your work. Isn't that stealing from your employers?

YETTA: I did open that door—

MRS. PANNO: God created levels for all men to have their dwelling. If each kept to the level intended for them, there would be peace.

YETTA: There might be peace, but there wouldn't be justice.

MRS. PANNO: It's for God to know what justice is.

YETTA: Well, let me think on that a while. Here's something for you to think about. Everybody hates you, Providenza. Everyone. Most are kinder about it than I. I can't get past my conviction that there's too little time to show kindness to those who are not kind, who don't even think it is their place to be kind. The rulers of the world with their hands so full things fall out of them, and then they resent it when we come behind them, picking the leavings up. What you have to think about is this: whether we hate you because you're the righteous upholder of natural order and barbarians like us can't abide that, or because you're the greedy and hateful tool of greedy and hateful oppressors. A Cossack. Let me know what you decide.

> *There's a stir in the hall, and one by one the girls come through the door, chattering, mostly about how lovely the children are.*

ESSIE: *(Ironically, in light of the above)* So beautiful, the little girls, and such beautiful clothes!

LUCIA: The girls on Eight made them. Mrs. Blanck brought in the little patterns and—

YETTA: Did they get paid?

GUSSIE: Oh, it was such an honor that—

ESSIE: Mrs. Panno! We missed you upstairs.

MRS. PANNO: Oh, I've seen the children before. I mean, socially. I have been to their house. Mr. Blanck wanted me to…do… something else.

YETTA: Mrs. Panno was down here checking to see what we had stolen from the Company.

MRS. PANNO: Oh, that's putting it a little—

ROSARIA: We can't get out the door at night without some smelly man pawing through our pocketbooks and making us show the tops of our stockings and—

MRS. PANNO: So I have been reminded.

LUCIA: So. What did you find?

Pause.

MRS. PANNO: Nothing. Nothing that couldn't be explained.

LUCIA: Sorry you had to waste your employers' time. Maybe next time there'll be contraband.

ROSARIA: We'll shove it in *culo* and you can look for it there.

Panno is hurt and tearing up.

MRS. PANNO: We all have our jobs to do.

LUCIA: —said Judas to Jesus.

MRS. PANNO: We all want the same. I guess we do. We want a ladder to climb up. Everything in our lives and the lives of our people back as far as we remember dug us the same hole, and we want out of it. Well, I found a way out. I found a way out where I didn't have to change the whole world. They said "do this" and I did it, and I was not chained to a sewing machine anymore. I showed respect to people I thought were respectable, because they were successful and what reason did I have to think those qualities would be at odds? I did what I thought was right, and it came out right. I know you hate me, but I don't know why. I have nothing but what you want to have, am nothing but what you want to be. A little better, a little more. I took only me, I know. Is that it? Nobody back then said you had to take everybody or it didn't count. I missed the meetings, Yetta. But I dirtied nothing, shattered nothing, changed nothing, knocked no one off the ladder before or behind. I would think someone would be proud of me—you maybe, one of you—for getting out of the hole without ever raising my voice. I'm sorry to be hated. I am. But God did not come to me in the middle of the night and point to one way or the other. I thought I was alone, so that's how I went. I really didn't know...

> *Panno sighs, gathers herself and marches grandly out. She returns briefly to gather up the handkerchief and lorgnette, which she left on the table after her dramatic moment. Exits. The girls stare after her. There is a quite long pause, into which Avi eases himself, tentatively. He is carrying a dish or bowl under a white cloth.*

AVI: Did somebody die? *(No response)* Mrs. Panno was sobbing in the corridor, so I thought maybe—

YETTA: We took a joke too far.

AVI: Didn't look like it was that funny. Anyway, the kids have had their cake and punch and the little girl in yellow vomited right over the side onto the street and Mrs. Blanck told me to get rid of this before it draws flies.

He lifts off the cloth to reveal an impressive quantity of sliced cake.

LUCIA: It's so—white.

AVI: Dig in, girls.
(They do)
She was right! It does draw flies!

Rosaria kisses him on the cheek.

ROSARIA: *Grazie, mio bello.*

AVI: *Preggo. (To Lucia)* How do you say "Marry me"?

LUCIA: I'm not telling you that for weeks yet.

AVI: Lucia—

LUCIA: My sister is FOURTEEN.

AVI: I am fifteen! I am a man! And I am at my best right this minute. I may not be bringing cake at another time.

LUCIA: You'll just have to think of something else.

ESSIE: A man! I'll bet there isn't a single hair on his balls.

Essie thinks she was whispering, but Avi overheard.

AVI: *(Sweetly)* You could come over here and check—

Playful swat of Avi by Essie. Rosaria picks up on the intimacy and moves subtly but firmly between them. Ad lib happy cake-eating chit-chat for a moment or two. Then:

GUSSIE: Essie, slow down, the sugar will go right to your head.

ESSIE: That's what I want it to do. Wine last night. White cake this afternoon.

YETTA: *(Sotto voce)* Avi's balls—

ESSIE: A sky like...I don't know what. And I saw ghosts on the roof but it was only birds and I don't want it to be over! I want to be giddy and fall down on the floor and see stars whirling above me.

GUSSIE: You had *wine*?

ESSIE: Just a sip from Reuben's cup. Everything was so perfect.

GUSSIE: A sip from Reuben's cup. That's practically marriage.

LUCIA: If you don't ask for too much, the year gives you just so many perfect days.

GUSSIE: Not that many.

LUCIA: It doesn't have to be that many.

ROSARIA: *Uno, due, tres—basta.*

YETTA: Two hours to the bell. I almost think I can make it.

AVI: Maybe this is one of those perfect days. We'll all wake up tomorrow and think "wasn't that wonderful?" There was cake, and Avi sang a song. Tomorrow could be awful, but it would still be all right for a little while. We'd find a white crumb in our shirt pocket and it'll all come back to us.

LUCIA: *(Gripping her belly)* Oh!

ESSIE: What is it?

YETTA: Too much cake?

GUSSIE: It isn't morning anymore—

YETTA: Look, we're not going to see Panno for a while. If you have to go, go now. We'll watch the corridor for you.

LUCIA: No, it's not that! She's quickening. I can feel her kicking in my womb. Oh, come feel—
(The girls rush over to feel the baby kicking: exclamations and happy giggling)
Avi, you come too.

Avi comes over and feels her belly. The baby kicks. A smile covers Avi's face.

AVI: *Bambina brava.*

LUCIA: *Si, si, si.*

ROSARIA: *(To Avi) Mio bello zio.*

GUSSIE: How can you know it's a girl?

LUCIA: When Mario was inside me, giving me the baby, he closed his eyes and said, "I see a beautiful girl, beautiful as her mother." That's how I know. Mario gave me a daughter.

ESSIE: Most men want sons.

LUCIA: Mario is not most men.

Pause while they stare at her. The scene should be as Madonna-like as possible.

YETTA: May she be born into a different world.

ALL: Amen. *(The Jewish girls and the Italian girls will pronounce this differently)*

AVI: Lucia, could Mario get me a job at the docks?

LUCIA: It would put shoulders on you just like he has.

AVI: I'd love to work down by the water. This is no job for a man.

ESSIE: But you're so pretty pushing the broom—

LUCIA: I'll see what I can do. You being almost family and all.

At this concession, Avi grins a wide grin.

YETTA: We could make that world for her. A better world for Lucia's daughter—
(General groan)
Don't groan at me. We could make sure she is born into a better world. We could. It wouldn't be so hard…we'd have to organize… we'd need to…

GUSSIE: Yetta, it's almost quitting time. Let me go home this one time without a headache.

ESSIE: Let *us* make the argument this time. We've heard it so much we can say it in our sleep. I'll be the greedy Capitalist all dressed in pretty clothes and Avi here will be the fiery revolutionary, who—

LUCIA: Yetta, I wish I was as smart as you. But I think you forget something. You forget that every moment of life is a gift and a surprise. It's not always what we want. I know that. But it's always—something, and often enough it's something wonderful. Sometimes it's so wonderful you would never have thought to ask. I know things should be better and that kind and good people must work for that, and I want my daughter to have better than me, and better, and better. But even so, it is all so beautiful All so *interesting.*

> *Pause.*

YETTA: *(Peeved)* You know I say the things I do out of love.

ESSIE: If we know that it's because you just now told us—

YETTA: Gussie—

GUSSIE: *(After a resistant pause)* All right. Yes. Yes. Out of love. I who have known you the longest know that...you are assured that you say what you say out of...some kind of love...only you can fully understand. Even though you snub me on the train, I will accept that you love all universally and unselfishly. Now let me finish a last few pieces so I can afford something for the baby shower.

> *After a few minutes of only the working of fingers and machines, Rosaria sings, without looking up from her work.*

ROSARIA:
Lascia la spina
cogli la rosa;
tu vai cercando
tu vai cercando
il tuo dolor.

Lascia la spina
cogli la rosa;
tu vai cercando
il tuo dolor.

It is, of course, Handel, but it is sung with awesome simplicity, like a folk song. They listen rapt. She finishes. Avi exits, kissing Rosaria on the top of her head. They go back to their work.

SCENE FIVE

It's nearly four in the afternoon. Lights come up on a scene of the women still at work, some of them stretching, staring off into space, fussing with a shirtwaist. From the distance, as through an open window, comes the sound of an organ grinder or concertina playing Rosaria's song or some other Italian classic. Rosaria la-las along a little bit.

YETTA: Sing some of it, Rosie

ROSARIA: No, no words. Too late in the afternoon. Just the tune. *Come gli uccelli.* I can't open my mouth wide enough for whole words to come out.

GUSSIE: It must be tomorrow by now.

LUCIA: I can hardly keep my eyes open.

ESSIE: I'm glad there's no clock in here. I'd never look at anything else.

YETTA: *(Sarcastic)* But we've been having so much fun! Pushing the fabric, pulling the fabric, cutting the thread...

ESSIE: It hasn't been the worst of days.

LUCIA: Some days go so slow. Other days are—

ESSIE: —less slow—

YETTA: That little adventure with the children put us behind.

LUCIA: Let it go, Yetta.

ROSARIA: I'm so—

ESSIE: I swear if none of us mentions how tired we are it will be perfection.

YETTA: We do talk about that a lot.

GUSSIE: It is the central fact of our existence.

ESSIE: And now it's my fault we can't talk about it.

GUSSIE: We could talk about men.

ESSIE: Fashion.

LUCIA: Babies.

ROSARIA: Love.

YETTA: Politics.

ESSIE: Coney Island.

YETTA: Pay day.

ESSIE: Pay day. Yes. Oh, where is that stupid boy?

ROSARIA: He can come only as fast as they give him the envelopes.

YETTA: He brings us cake, he brings us money. When I think of God now he has Avi's smiling face.

ESSIE: God doesn't sing as much.

LUCIA: *(Rising and stretching)* In half an hour that bell will ring and we will be free.

GUSSIE: Imagine if you didn't have to come right back tomorrow.

ESSIE: Maybe we won't. All sorts of things could happen between today and tomorrow.

GUSSIE: Mr. Rockefeller might come calling. "Mama just ask him to wait until I freshen up a little—"

YETTA: Maybe I'll marry a gypsy and go to Paris. Are there still gypsies?

GUSSIE: Is the gypsy named Theodore?

YETTA: I swear to God, Gussie, if you breathe one word—

ESSIE: Theodore? What? The blond boy upstairs?

YETTA: *(To Gussie)* Your life hangs in the balance—

LUCIA: Mrs. Panno hasn't come back. Maybe we hurt her feelings.

GUSSIE: She never lingers on payday. She hates to see us happy.

> *Suddenly Avi enters like a swashbuckler in the recently popular movies. He bears in hand a sheaf of pay packets.*

AVI: Who do we love more than anybody else in the world?

ALL: You!

GUSSIE: But only when you have pay packets in your hand.

LUCIA: We'll forget you one minute after the money is in our hands.

General hubbub and anticipation. With great ceremony, and reading the names on the packets as though he'd never heard of them before, he hands the money out. The women receive the packets and each puts it into her own secret place—the top of one's stocking, another's cleavage, another in a secret pocket in her skirt, etc.

AVI: Lucia Maltese.
   (She comes and gets it, hides it away)
Gussie Bierman.
   (As above)
Albina Caruso.

LUCIA: I'll take hers. She lives in my building.

AVI: I'm not supposed to—

LUCIA: *(Holding out her hand commandingly)* Give!

   He does.

AVI: Yetta Goldstein.
   (The same)
Rosaria Maltese.
   (She approaches, he holds the envelope above her head)
I'll need a little something in return.

   He withholds the packet until she kisses him. Gussie suddenly jumps away from her machine.

GUSSIE: Oh!

YETTA: What is it?

GUSSIE: It's—the electric...the electric bit me.

LUCIA: Well, that woke me up—

YETTA: It's a short or something. I'll tell Mr. Blanck at the door as we leave.

ESSIE: Make him come tinker with it first so he gets a big shock.

LUCIA: I wish we hadn't seen him with his children. It makes him harder to hate.

ESSIE: We'll forget the children by and by.

AVI: Essie Bernstein.
   (She approaches, he teases)
It says here on the envelope that Essie has been a nasty and hateful girl who says bad things about the young and innocent. So she must work a little harder for her pay this week.

ESSIE: *(Reaching for the packet)* Give!

AVI: Don't you agree there should be a penalty?

ALL: *(Variations on)* Yes! A penalty!

AVI: I think she should sing for her supper.

ALL: *(Variations on)* Yes!

GUSSIE: She goes to all the music halls with Reuben the *Tchotchka*-Bestower. Give her something hard.

AVI: *(Sings) Du bist dos likht fun mayne oygn*—you now! You!

ESSIE: You said it was going to be hard— *(Sings) Nor du bashaynst mayn velt far mir*

AVI: *(Sings) Du host mikh tsu zikh tsugetsoygn*

ESSIE: *(Sings) Az lebn ken ikh nit on dir—*

Wild applause. All the Jewish girls join in, all the Italian girls clap.

ESSIE, YETTA, GUSSIE: *(Sing)*
Du makst mayn nakht zol likhtik vern
Dem bloyen himel brengstu mir
Du mist mayn heller—

A blast of smoke issues from the area of Gussie's machine. Fire leaps from her scrap bin, from the machine, rolling red and gold into the corners of the room. The girls run screaming toward the door. Suddenly, they freeze in attitudes of fear and flight, except for Yetta.

YETTA: Theodore, with his yellow hair. That's what I though of. It is him I want. I knew when I saw the flame come onto Gussie's skirt. I knew it then. The fire speaking...about how things tie together...there is no way to understand. He is upstairs. Running. His door is sealed too. I see us with red banners in our hands, in the middle of the street, marching. We are dressed in red. Everything is red. They are crying...all the world above and all the world below us are crying. It is him I want. Despite whatever happens. I must go to tell him. I am moving to the door. I cannot move.

The mayhem starts again, in a second freezes again, this time for Lucia.

LUCIA: *(Cradling her unborn baby)* Sweetheart, go to papa. Fly to him. He loves you. Leave me. Leave me. Be turned to air! Be turned to a flower. Snow white. Indestructible. Oh, sweet Jesus, give her wings. Fly away...fly away...

In a flash, it's mayhem again. The women are gone. The lights grow intenser, until the room is blindingly blood red. Their screams are augmented by the screams of others elsewhere in the building. There is the roaring of flames, the crashing of ceilings and fixtures, the distant clanging of fire truck bells. The din dies a little, and the red, though still ubiquitous, is less intense. The music of the tune they were singing—played klezmer or on a concertina—drifts in above the mayhem. Avi enters. As Avi speaks, the women enter again, slowly, and stand in the red light as in a fire.

AVI: It was over in eighteen minutes. One hundred forty-six died. Doors and stairwells had been locked to prevent pilferage and unauthorized breaks. The one usable door opened in, so when forty or fifty frantic bodies were pressed against it, it could not be opened. There was one fire escape, and, rusty and shoddy, it collapsed almost immediately. Zito the elevator man did his best, but the elevator cables warped with the heat, and people fought their way out of the stalled elevator to die in the shaft below. When it was clear the corridor was hopeless, people ran to the windows, the eighth, ninth, tenth floors. Some who were not ready to jump were pushed out by people afire behind them. Flaming bodies crashed onto the pavement, where the firemen, who were helpless to reach the fire so far up, put them out with their hoses. Greene Street was closed because of the danger of being hit by falling bodies. I ran up. I must have remembered what she said. Mrs. Panno saved me. I ran up, and the doors up were open. I was screaming for Rosaria, but I didn't know how to find her. All the girls looked like her, and none of them did. The girls' hair was on fire, and their clothes streamed fire behind them as they ran. I tried to pull them upstairs with me. I couldn't understand why more didn't come. I guess they wanted to get to the street, where they could run. I was afraid. I didn't try hard enough. A few girls and Mr. Blanck and his wife and their children made it to the roof. So few, I thought. Why didn't anybody know to go up? They thought they were going to burn to death unless they got into the open, even if it was empty air. I was not going to burn to death. There was a shed on the roof. I ripped it apart with my hands and began laying the planks from our roof to the roof of the college next door. Mr. Blanck caught on and helped me, and the children and the women got over, and then we did. All under us was fire and screaming, and the thump of bodies hitting pavement. Eighteen minutes. They were gone, all of them. The baby in Lucia's belly became a little scarlet rose, and then was gone. Rosaria was gone. Mrs. Panno forgot what she knew, and never came to the roof. All those plans made nothing. All those conversations stopped. The nighthawks were flying over the roof, crying. So many bodies piled against the foundation that I had to wait a day to get back in my room. I looked to see if Rosaria was among them. I'd know her even if she turned to coal. No. Not even that. *Mia cara, addio.*

Avi exits. The women lit by the blood red light stand looking out at the audience for as long as it can be stood. Then the lights come down.

About the Author

David Brendan Hopes is a poet, a playwright, and an author of fiction and nonfiction prose. His theatrical works have been produced in New York, Chicago, Los Angeles, and regionally, including Asheville, NC, where he lives. He has twice received the North Carolina New Play Project Prize, as well as the Holland New Voices Playwriting Award, the Sprenger Foundation Award for Historical Drama, the Desert Star Award for Best Original Writing, the Arch and Bruce Brown Foundation Award for Playwriting, and the Siena Playwrights' Prize. Poetry accolades include the Juniper Prize and the Saxifrage Prize. Originally from Ohio, Hopes taught at Hiram College, Syracuse University, Phillips Exeter Academy, and the University of North Carolina at Asheville. His published novels include *The Falls of Wyona,* which won the Quill Prize from Red Hen Press; *Night, Sleep and The Dreams of Lovers*; and *The One with the Beautiful Necklaces.* His nature essays, "A Sense of the Morning" and "Birdsongs of the Mesozoic," appeared from Milkweed Editions and his memoir, *A Childhood in the Milky Way,* from Akron University Press.

www.ingramcontent.com/pod-product-compliance
Lightning Source LLC
Chambersburg PA
CBHW030349100526
44592CB00010B/883